Shadows of Secrecy: Espionage and Intelligence in the Manhattan Project

Table of Contents

Shadows of Secrecy: Espionage and Intelligence in the Manhattan Project

By Roberto Miguel Rodriguez

Chapter 1: The Manhattan Project: The Top-Secret Program That Produced the Atomic Bomb in World War II

The Origins of the Manhattan Project

The Manhattan Project, one of the most significant scientific endeavors in history, had its origins in the geopolitical landscape of the early 20th century. As the world plunged into the depths of World War II, the race to develop atomic weapons became a matter of utmost importance for the major powers involved. This subchapter delves into the intriguing origins of the Manhattan Project, shedding light on the key events and individuals that set the stage for this top-secret program.

The genesis of the Manhattan Project can be traced back to the scientific breakthroughs of the early 20th century. Albert Einstein's theory of relativity sparked a profound transformation in the field of physics, laying the groundwork for the theoretical understanding of atomic energy. Scientists like Enrico Fermi, Leo Szilard, and J. Robert Oppenheimer were among those captivated by the potential of harnessing this energy for military purposes.

However, it was the geopolitical climate of the time that truly catalyzed the Manhattan Project. With the rise of Nazi Germany and the fear that they may be developing atomic weapons, many prominent scientists, many of whom were Jewish refugees fleeing persecution, felt an urgent need to ensure that the United States remained at the forefront of this scientific race.

In response to these concerns, the United States government established the Manhattan Project in 1939 under the leadership of General Leslie Groves. The project operated under a shroud of secrecy, with its true nature hidden from the public and even many of those involved. The primary goal was to develop an atomic bomb before Germany could achieve the same, thus ensuring American superiority in the war.

Scientists from various disciplines, including physics, chemistry, and engineering, were recruited to work on different aspects of the project. Facilities were established in remote locations such as Los Alamos, New Mexico, to carry out the research and development necessary for the creation of the atomic bomb.

The decision to use the atomic bomb on Hiroshima and Nagasaki in 1945 marked a turning point in history and raised profound ethical and moral dilemmas. The long-term consequences, both environmental and political, of this decision are still being debated today.

The Manhattan Project not only had a significant impact on the outcome of World War II but also shaped the course of post-war international relations. It propelled the United States into a position of unmatched power and influence, leading to the Cold War and the subsequent arms race with the Soviet Union.

The legacy of the Manhattan Project continues to spark debates about the use of atomic weapons in warfare and the ethical responsibilities of scientists. As historians, it is crucial to explore the origins of this top-secret program to gain a comprehensive understanding of its wider implications and significance in shaping the world we live in today.

The Birth of the Atomic Age

The Birth of the Atomic Age marked a monumental turning point in human history, forever altering the course of warfare, science, and international relations. This subchapter delves into the inception and early days of the Manhattan Project, the top-secret program that produced the atomic bomb during World War II.

The Manhattan Project emerged against the backdrop of a world at war, where the race to harness the power of the atom became a matter of utmost urgency. Spearheaded by the United States, the project brought together a brilliant array of scientists, including the iconic Albert Einstein, whose groundbreaking theories had laid the foundation for atomic research.

Einstein's role in the Manhattan Project was primarily that of a moral compass, as he advocated for the project's development to prevent the Nazis from obtaining atomic weapons first. However, his involvement lent immense credibility to the scientific community's pursuit of this new and devastating technology.

The project was not without its ethical and moral dilemmas. Scientists grappled with the devastating potential of the atomic bomb and the implications of unleashing such destructive power upon humanity. Many faced internal conflicts as they weighed the necessity of their work against the potential loss of innocent lives.

The cloak of secrecy surrounding the Manhattan Project was of paramount importance, as spies and intelligence operations from foreign powers sought to obtain classified information. Espionage became a constant threat, heightening the tension and paranoia within the project's ranks.

The successful development of the atomic bomb by the Manhattan Project had profound consequences on the end of World War II. The bombings of Hiroshima and Nagasaki forced Japan's surrender, but also raised questions about the morality of using such destructive force on civilian populations.

The aftermath of the war brought about political and diplomatic implications that would shape post-war international relations. The United States emerged as a superpower, while the Soviet Union's desire to obtain atomic weapons ushered in the Cold War and the subsequent arms race.

The environmental consequences and long-term effects of the atomic bomb were also felt for generations to come. The devastation caused by the bombings forever altered the landscapes and left a lasting impact on the survivors.

The legacy of the Manhattan Project continues to provoke ongoing debates about the use of atomic weapons in warfare. Historians grapple with the ethical implications, questioning whether the ends justified the means. These discussions have shaped the way we view the use of nuclear power and its potential for both destruction and advancement.

In conclusion, the birth of the Atomic Age through the Manhattan Project unleashed unprecedented power and forever changed the world. The scientific breakthroughs, espionage operations, ethical dilemmas, and far-reaching consequences of this top-secret program continue to captivate historians, fuel ongoing debates, and shape the course of human history.

The Race to Develop Atomic Weapons

One of the most significant chapters in the history of warfare and scientific discovery is the race to develop atomic weapons during World War II. This subchapter will delve into the intense competition between the United States and Nazi Germany, highlighting the key moments and individuals that shaped the outcome of this race.

At the forefront of this race was the Manhattan Project, a top-secret program that brought together some of the world's most brilliant scientists. Led by prominent figures like J. Robert Oppenheimer and Enrico Fermi, the project aimed to harness the power of the atom for military purposes. This subchapter will explore the scientific discoveries and breakthroughs achieved by the Manhattan Project, shedding light on the revolutionary advancements that made atomic weapons a reality.

One of the key figures in the development of atomic weapons was Albert Einstein, whose theories laid the groundwork for the project. Einstein's involvement in the Manhattan Project will be examined, along with the contributions of other prominent scientists who grappled with the ethical and moral dilemmas surrounding their work. The subchapter will shed light on the profound implications of their choices and the internal conflicts faced by those involved.

Espionage and intelligence played a crucial role in this race, as both the United States and Nazi Germany sought to gather information about each other's progress. This subchapter will delve into the espionage operations surrounding the Manhattan Project, highlighting the key individuals and events that shaped the outcome of this race.

The impact of the Manhattan Project on the end of World War II cannot be overstated. The atomic bombs dropped on Hiroshima and Nagasaki brought about a swift conclusion to the war, but they also raised significant ethical and moral questions. This subchapter will explore the environmental consequences and long-term effects of the atomic bomb, as well as the post-war political and diplomatic implications for international relations.

The legacy of the Manhattan Project extended far beyond World War II. This subchapter will examine its influence on the Cold War and the subsequent arms race between the United States and the Soviet Union. The ongoing debates surrounding the Manhattan Project and the use of atomic weapons in warfare will also be explored, highlighting the lasting impact and continuing relevance of this pivotal moment in history.

In conclusion, the race to develop atomic weapons during World War II was a defining chapter in human history. This subchapter will provide historians with a comprehensive account of this race, its key players, and the far-reaching consequences that are still felt to this day.

Secrecy and Security Measures

The Manhattan Project, one of the most secretive and high-stakes scientific endeavors in history, demanded unprecedented levels of secrecy and security. In this subchapter, we delve into the complex web of measures put in place to protect the project's classified information and ensure its scientific breakthroughs remained hidden from enemy spies.

At the heart of the project's secrecy efforts was the need for compartmentalization. Scientists and engineers were divided into smaller teams, with each group working on a specific aspect of the project without knowledge of the overall objective. This approach minimized the risk of leaks and prevented a complete understanding of the project's scope by any single individual.

Physical security measures were also paramount. The project's research sites, such as Los Alamos and Oak Ridge, were tightly guarded, with armed personnel and restricted access points. Security clearances were required for anyone involved, and background checks were extensive. Each person had to go through multiple levels of vetting to ensure their loyalty and reliability.

To further safeguard against espionage, the project established a counterintelligence program. This program employed skilled agents to identify and neutralize potential threats. Suspicious activities, unauthorized access attempts, or suspicious communications were closely monitored, and informants were cultivated to gather intelligence on potential spies or leaks.

The project also relied on cryptography to protect its communications. Messages were encrypted using complex codes and ciphers, making it nearly impossible for unauthorized individuals to decipher the contents.

The use of code names and pseudonyms further obscured the true identities of those involved in the project.

The consequences of failure in maintaining secrecy were severe. Espionage and leaks had the potential to compromise the entire project, jeopardizing the United States' efforts to develop atomic weapons ahead of Nazi Germany. The fear of leaks and spies heightened the ethical and moral dilemmas faced by the scientists, forcing them to grapple with the implications of their work.

The stringent secrecy and security measures put in place during the Manhattan Project were successful in preventing any major breaches. This allowed the project to proceed unhindered and ultimately led to the successful development of the atomic bomb. However, the legacy of secrecy and its impact on post-war international relations, the environment, and the ongoing debates about the use of atomic weapons remains a topic of critical importance and ongoing discussion among historians and scholars.

Chapter 2: The Scientific Discoveries and Breakthroughs of the Manhattan Project

Theoretical Foundations of Nuclear Physics

Theoretical Foundations of Nuclear Physics is a subchapter in the book "Shadows of Secrecy: Espionage and Intelligence in the Manhattan Project." This chapter delves into the scientific principles and concepts that laid the groundwork for the development of atomic weapons during World War II. It aims to provide historians with a comprehensive understanding of the key theories and discoveries that shaped the Manhattan Project.

The subchapter begins by exploring the scientific breakthroughs that paved the way for nuclear physics. It delves into the works of prominent scientists such as Albert Einstein, Enrico Fermi, and J. Robert Oppenheimer, who played crucial roles in developing the theoretical foundations of nuclear physics. It discusses the revolutionary theories of relativity and quantum mechanics and their impact on understanding the behavior of particles at the atomic level.

The chapter then delves into the specific principles of nuclear physics that were essential for the Manhattan Project. It explores the concept of nuclear fission, which was first discovered by Otto Hahn and Fritz Strassmann in 1938. This breakthrough paved the way for harnessing the immense energy released during the splitting of an atomic nucleus.

The subchapter also explores the process of chain reactions and critical mass, which were vital for sustaining a self-sustaining nuclear reaction. It discusses the role of neutron moderators and control rods in regulating the rate of the reaction, highlighting the intricate scientific understanding required for harnessing nuclear energy for destructive purposes.

Furthermore, the subchapter examines the scientific challenges faced by the scientists involved in the Manhattan Project. It highlights the ethical and moral dilemmas they encountered as they realized the potentially devastating consequences of their discoveries. It also explores the ongoing debates surrounding the use of atomic weapons in warfare and the legacy of the Manhattan Project.

Overall, this subchapter provides a comprehensive overview of the theoretical foundations of nuclear physics that underpinned the development of atomic weapons during the Manhattan Project. It offers historians valuable insights into the scientific principles, breakthroughs, and ethical dilemmas faced by the scientists involved, shedding light on the complex and multifaceted history of this groundbreaking program.

The Discovery of Nuclear Fission

The discovery of nuclear fission stands as one of the most significant scientific breakthroughs in history, and it played a pivotal role in the development of the atomic bomb during World War II. This subchapter delves into the intricate details of this discovery, shedding light on the scientists involved, the ethical dilemmas they faced, and the subsequent impact on international relations.

In 1938, Otto Hahn and Fritz Strassmann, two German chemists, made a ground-breaking observation while conducting experiments with uranium. They discovered that bombarding uranium atoms with neutrons caused them to split into smaller atoms, releasing an enormous amount of energy. This process, known as nuclear fission, was a revolutionary finding that laid the foundation for the development of atomic weapons.

News of this discovery quickly spread throughout the scientific community, capturing the attention of prominent scientists such as Albert Einstein and Leo Szilard. Recognizing the potential for harnessing this energy for destructive purposes, they sent a letter to President Franklin D. Roosevelt, urging him to initiate a research program that would ultimately become the Manhattan Project.

However, the discovery of nuclear fission also presented scientists with profound ethical and moral dilemmas. Many scientists grappled with the implications of their work, questioning the devastating consequences that could result from the use of atomic weapons. This subchapter explores the internal conflicts faced by these scientists and the decisions they made in the pursuit of scientific progress.

Moreover, the discovery of nuclear fission sparked a race between the United States and Nazi Germany to develop atomic weapons. This subchapter delves into the espionage and intelligence operations surrounding the Manhattan Project, highlighting the efforts made by both sides to gather classified information and sabotage their adversaries' progress.

The impact of the Manhattan Project on the end of World War II cannot be overstated. The atomic bombs dropped on Hiroshima and Nagasaki forced Japan's surrender, but they also unleashed unimaginable destruction and suffering. This subchapter explores the political and diplomatic implications of this devastating event, shaping post-war international relations and paving the way for the Cold War.

Furthermore, the environmental consequences and long-term effects of the atomic bomb are examined, as the legacy of the Manhattan Project continues to raise ongoing debates regarding the use of atomic weapons in warfare. This subchapter provides historians with a comprehensive understanding of the scientific, ethical, political, and moral dimensions surrounding the discovery of nuclear fission and its subsequent impact on the world.

Harnessing the Power of the Atom

The Manhattan Project stands as one of the most significant scientific endeavors of the 20th century. In the subchapter "Harnessing the Power of the Atom," we delve into the incredible scientific discoveries and breakthroughs that shaped the project, the role of prominent scientists such as Albert Einstein, and the ethical and moral dilemmas faced by those involved.

At its core, the Manhattan Project aimed to develop an atomic bomb, utilizing the power of nuclear fission. The scientific community harnessed the immense potential of the atom, pushing the boundaries of knowledge and technology. This subchapter explores the intricate scientific processes involved, from the discovery of uranium's fissionability to the construction of complex reactors and the separation of isotopes.

Central to the project's success was the collaboration of brilliant minds like Albert Einstein, who played a crucial role in both inspiring and advocating for atomic research. Einstein's letter to President Franklin D. Roosevelt, warning of the potential for Nazi Germany to develop atomic weapons, set the wheels in motion for the top-secret program.

Yet, the scientists involved faced profound ethical and moral dilemmas throughout the Manhattan Project. As they pushed forward with their research, they grappled with the devastating potential of their discoveries. The subchapter highlights the personal struggles faced by scientists such as J. Robert Oppenheimer, who famously questioned the morality of their work in creating such destructive weapons.

Espionage and intelligence operations also played a significant role in the Manhattan Project. The subchapter delves into the clandestine efforts of both the United States and Nazi Germany to obtain crucial information on atomic research. It uncovers the web of intrigue and the race against time that unfolded behind the scenes.

The impact of the Manhattan Project on World War II cannot be understated. The atomic bombs dropped on Hiroshima and Nagasaki brought about the swift end of the war, but at a tremendous cost. This subchapter explores the decision-making process behind the use of these weapons and the ongoing debates surrounding their necessity.

Moreover, the subchapter delves into the long-term consequences of the atomic bomb, both environmentally and politically. It discusses the devastating effects on the environment and the subsequent efforts to mitigate nuclear fallout. It also examines the political and diplomatic implications of the Manhattan Project on post-war international relations and its role in shaping the Cold War and the arms race between the United States and the Soviet Union.

As historians, we must recognize the legacy of the Manhattan Project and the ongoing debates surrounding the use of atomic weapons in warfare. This subchapter offers a comprehensive exploration of this pivotal moment in history, shedding light on the scientific achievements, ethical dilemmas, espionage operations, and the far-reaching consequences that continue to shape our world today.

Scientific Challenges and Innovations

The Manhattan Project was a top-secret program that produced the atomic bomb during World War II, and it stands as one of the most significant scientific achievements in human history. Within this chapter, we will explore the scientific challenges and innovations that were instrumental in the success of this project.

At its core, the Manhattan Project relied on groundbreaking scientific discoveries and breakthroughs. Physicists such as Albert Einstein, Enrico Fermi, and J. Robert Oppenheimer played pivotal roles in developing the theories and technologies that made the atomic bomb possible. Their work revolutionized our understanding of nuclear particles, fission reactions, and the immense energy that could be harnessed from splitting an atom.

However, these scientific advancements did not come without their challenges. The project faced numerous obstacles, including the need for a reliable source of enriched uranium and the construction of massive industrial facilities to support the research and development efforts. Overcoming these obstacles required innovative solutions and collaborations between scientists, engineers, and industrialists.

One of the most significant scientific challenges was the creation of a sustainable nuclear chain reaction. Achieving this required the design and construction of a complex apparatus known as a nuclear reactor. The scientists involved in the project had to overcome technical hurdles and address safety concerns to ensure the controlled release of energy from the fission process.

As the project progressed, the ethical and moral dilemmas faced by the scientists involved became increasingly apparent. The realization that the atomic bomb could cause immense destruction and loss of life forced them to grapple with the consequences of their work. This chapter will delve into the debates and discussions that took place among these scientists as they wrestled with their role in shaping the outcome of the war.

In addition to the scientific challenges, the Manhattan Project was also surrounded by espionage and intelligence operations. Both the United States and Nazi Germany were in a race to develop atomic weapons, and the project became a target for foreign spies. This subchapter will explore the covert activities that took place and their impact on the project's success.

The scientific innovations and challenges faced during the Manhattan Project had far-reaching implications beyond World War II. The atomic bomb ultimately played a decisive role in ending the war, but it also had significant political, diplomatic, and environmental consequences. This chapter will examine the long-term effects of the atomic bomb and its influence on post-war international relations, the Cold War, and the arms race between the United States and the Soviet Union.

Even today, the legacy of the Manhattan Project remains a subject of ongoing debate. The use of atomic weapons in warfare raises profound moral and ethical questions, and this chapter will explore the continuing discussions surrounding the project and its impact on the world.

For historians interested in the Manhattan Project and its scientific, political, and moral dimensions, this subchapter offers an in-depth exploration of the challenges faced and the innovations achieved during this groundbreaking endeavor.

Chapter 3: The Role of Albert Einstein and Other Prominent Scientists in the Manhattan Project

Einstein's Influence on the Project

Albert Einstein, the renowned physicist and Nobel laureate, played a significant role in the Manhattan Project, the top-secret program that produced the atomic bomb during World War II. Einstein's scientific discoveries and breakthroughs, along with his political activism, had a profound impact on the project.

Einstein's involvement in the Manhattan Project started with a letter he wrote to President Franklin D. Roosevelt in 1939, warning him of the potential military applications of nuclear fission. This letter, known as the Einstein-Szilard letter, urged the United States to begin research on atomic weapons. Although Einstein did not directly participate in the project, his letter was instrumental in convincing the government to take action.

Einstein's influence extended beyond his initial letter. His scientific insights and expertise were crucial in the development of the theoretical framework necessary for the project's success. Scientists working on the Manhattan Project often sought his advice and guidance, relying on his deep understanding of physics and his innovative thinking.

Moreover, Einstein's moral and ethical stance on the use of atomic weapons had a profound impact on the scientists involved in the project. Einstein was a vocal critic of war and violence, and he was deeply concerned about the devastating consequences of atomic warfare. He feared that the use of the atomic bomb would lead to a dangerous arms race and the potential annihilation of humankind.

Einstein's influence on the project's ethical and moral dilemmas was evident in the debates and discussions among the scientists. Many scientists grappled with the ethical implications of their work, wrestling with the question of whether the bomb should be used against the Axis powers. Einstein's voice, along with other prominent scientists such as Leo Szilard and Robert Oppenheimer, played a crucial role in shaping these discussions.

In the aftermath of the project's success, Einstein continued to advocate for international control of atomic weapons. He became a prominent figure in the nuclear disarmament movement, warning of the dangers of nuclear proliferation and urging world leaders to pursue peaceful means of resolving conflicts.

Einstein's influence on the Manhattan Project extended beyond its immediate impact on World War II. His involvement set the stage for the subsequent Cold War and the arms race between the United States and the Soviet Union. The legacy of the project and ongoing debates surrounding the use of atomic weapons in warfare continue to be shaped by Einstein's contributions and his unwavering commitment to peace.

In conclusion, Einstein's influence on the Manhattan Project cannot be overstated. His scientific insights, political activism, and moral convictions had a profound impact on the development and ethical considerations of the project. Einstein's involvement in the Manhattan Project remains a significant aspect of his legacy and continues to shape the ongoing debates surrounding the use of atomic weapons in warfare.

The Scientific Brain Trust

One of the most remarkable aspects of the Manhattan Project was the gathering of the scientific brain trust that occurred during the early 1940s. This subchapter explores the prominent scientists who played a pivotal role in the top-secret program that produced the atomic bomb in World War II.

Led by physicist J. Robert Oppenheimer, the scientific team consisted of some of the brightest minds of the time. Albert Einstein, although not directly involved in the project, had a significant impact on its inception. His letter to President Franklin D. Roosevelt in 1939 warning about the potential for Nazi Germany to develop atomic weapons prompted the establishment of the Manhattan Project.

Einstein's insight and reputation attracted other eminent scientists to the project. Enrico Fermi, a Nobel laureate in physics, joined the team and made groundbreaking contributions to the development of a sustainable nuclear chain reaction. Physicists Niels Bohr and Leo Szilard also played key roles in advancing the scientific understanding behind the atomic bomb.

The scientific discoveries and breakthroughs made during the Manhattan Project were truly revolutionary. The team successfully harnessed the power of nuclear fission, unlocking the potential for immense destructive power. They achieved the first controlled nuclear reaction and, ultimately, the creation of the atomic bomb.

However, the ethical and moral dilemmas faced by the scientists involved cannot be understated. Many of them grappled with the implications of their work and the devastating consequences of the atomic bomb. Oppenheimer, in particular, expressed regret and remorse after witnessing the destructive power of the bomb in Hiroshima and Nagasaki.

The espionage and intelligence operations surrounding the Manhattan Project added another layer of complexity. Soviet spies infiltrated the project, gathering vital information that contributed to the Soviet Union's own development of atomic weapons. The impact of this intelligence breach on post-war international relations cannot be ignored.

The Manhattan Project's legacy extends far beyond World War II. It directly influenced the Cold War and the arms race between the United States and the Soviet Union. The project's success set the stage for the development of even more powerful nuclear weapons and ushered in an era of unprecedented global tension.

To this day, the Manhattan Project remains a source of ongoing debates and controversy. The use of atomic weapons in warfare and the potential for catastrophic destruction continue to be subjects of intense scrutiny. Historians continue to explore the complex political, diplomatic, and environmental implications of this top-secret program, shedding light on the lasting consequences of the scientific brain trust that emerged during the Manhattan Project.

The Collaborative Efforts of Scientists

In the race to develop atomic weapons during World War II, the Manhattan Project stands as a testament to the power of collaborative efforts among scientists. This subchapter explores the incredible teamwork and dedication that went into the scientific discoveries and breakthroughs of this top-secret program.

The Manhattan Project brought together some of the greatest scientific minds of the time, including Albert Einstein and other prominent scientists. These individuals, driven by a sense of duty and an understanding of the potential consequences of their work, worked tirelessly to unlock the secrets of atomic energy.

The project's success hinged on the collaboration and exchange of ideas between scientists. They formed research teams and laboratories where they could share their findings and work together towards a common goal. This open atmosphere of collaboration allowed for rapid advancement and breakthroughs that would have been impossible for individual scientists working in isolation.

However, the collaborative efforts of scientists involved in the Manhattan Project were not without ethical and moral dilemmas. They were aware of the destructive power of the atomic bomb they were creating and faced internal debates about the implications of their work. Some scientists, like J. Robert Oppenheimer, wrestled with the ethical dilemma of whether the bomb should be used as a weapon of war.

The espionage and intelligence operations surrounding the Manhattan Project further highlight the collaborative nature of the endeavor. The project was shrouded in secrecy, and scientists worked closely with intelligence agencies to protect classified information from falling into the wrong hands. The successful collaboration between scientists and intelligence agencies ensured that vital information remained secure and contributed to the overall success of the project.

The impact of the Manhattan Project on the end of World War II cannot be overstated. The atomic bombs dropped on Hiroshima and Nagasaki brought about a swift and decisive end to the war, but they also raised important questions about the long-term effects and environmental consequences of such a devastating weapon.

The Manhattan Project's influence on post-war international relations and the Cold War cannot be ignored either. The successful development of atomic weapons by the United States had far-reaching political and diplomatic implications, leading to an arms race with the Soviet Union and shaping the global power dynamics for decades to come.

The collaborative efforts of scientists involved in the Manhattan Project continue to be a subject of ongoing debates and discussions. The legacy of the project raises important questions about the use of atomic weapons in warfare and the ethical responsibilities of scientists in times of war.

In conclusion, the collaborative efforts of scientists were at the heart of the Manhattan Project's success. Through their teamwork, dedication, and exchange of ideas, they achieved scientific breakthroughs that changed the course of history. However, this collaboration also presented scientists with ethical and moral dilemmas, and the consequences of their work continue to shape the world today.

Personal Sacrifices and Commitments

In the pursuit of scientific breakthroughs and the development of the atomic bomb during World War II, the individuals involved in the Manhattan Project made personal sacrifices and commitments that shaped the course of history. This subchapter delves into the stories of these individuals and explores the ethical dilemmas, intelligence operations, and political implications they faced.

The scientists and engineers working on the Manhattan Project were driven by a deep sense of patriotism and a belief in the necessity of creating a weapon that could end the war. Their commitment to the project meant long hours, grueling research, and minimal personal time. Many of these scientists were renowned figures, such as Albert Einstein, who played a crucial role in the initial stages of the project. Their dedication to the cause meant putting aside personal ambitions and sacrificing time with loved ones.

However, the personal sacrifices extended beyond time and relationships. The scientists faced profound ethical and moral dilemmas as they grappled with the consequences of their work. The development of the atomic bomb raised questions about the use of such a destructive weapon and the potential loss of innocent lives. These scientists were torn between their duty to their country and their responsibility to humanity.

Furthermore, the intelligence and espionage operations surrounding the Manhattan Project added another layer of sacrifice and commitment. The project was shrouded in secrecy, and the scientists were under constant surveillance to ensure no leaks occurred. They had to navigate a web of deception and secrecy, often unable to share their work with even their closest colleagues. This created a sense of isolation and loneliness, as they carried the weight of the project's success or failure on their shoulders.

The impact of the Manhattan Project on the end of World War II cannot be overstated. The atomic bomb played a decisive role in forcing Japan's surrender, but it also unleashed a new era of warfare. The environmental consequences and long-term effects of the atomic bomb continue to be debated to this day.

The Manhattan Project's legacy extends beyond the war, shaping post-war international relations, the Cold War, and the arms race between the United States and the Soviet Union. The project's influence on nuclear proliferation and the ongoing debates surrounding the use of atomic weapons in warfare persist.

Through personal sacrifices and unwavering commitments, the individuals involved in the Manhattan Project played a pivotal role in altering the course of history. Their stories shed light on the complex moral, ethical, and political dimensions of scientific discovery and its implications for humanity. As historians, it is our duty to delve into these personal sacrifices and commitments to gain a deeper understanding of this transformative period in history.

Chapter 4: The Ethical and Moral Dilemmas Faced by Scientists Involved in the Manhattan Project

The Debate over the Use of Atomic Weapons

The development and use of atomic weapons during World War II remains one of the most controversial and heavily debated topics in history. The Manhattan Project, a top-secret program that produced the atomic bomb, brought together brilliant scientists and engineers who worked tirelessly to harness the power of the atom. However, this unprecedented scientific achievement was not without its ethical, moral, and political dilemmas.

One of the key questions that emerged during the Manhattan Project was whether it was morally justifiable to use atomic weapons in warfare. Many scientists involved in the project, including Albert Einstein, expressed their concerns about the devastating impact of these weapons on civilian populations. They feared that the use of atomic bombs would unleash unparalleled destruction and suffering.

On the other hand, proponents of using atomic weapons argued that it was necessary to bring a swift end to the war and save countless lives. They believed that the use of these weapons would force Japan to surrender, thus avoiding a costly and protracted invasion of the Japanese mainland.

The decision to drop atomic bombs on Hiroshima and Nagasaki in August 1945 remains one of the most significant and controversial events of the war. While it did lead to Japan's surrender and the end of World War II, it also resulted in the deaths of hundreds of thousands of civilians and caused long-term environmental consequences.

The legacy of the Manhattan Project and the use of atomic weapons continued to shape post-war international relations. The United States emerged as the world's sole nuclear power, and the development of atomic weapons set the stage for the Cold War and the arms race between the United States and the Soviet Union.

Today, the ongoing debate over the use of atomic weapons in warfare remains relevant and contentious. Scholars and historians continue to grapple with the ethical implications of using such devastating weapons, as well as the long-term environmental and human effects.

The shadows of secrecy that surrounded the Manhattan Project continue to intrigue and captivate historians, as they seek to understand the scientific discoveries, breakthroughs, and espionage that characterized this top-secret program. By examining the role of prominent scientists like Albert Einstein, the political and diplomatic implications, and the lasting legacies of the Manhattan Project, historians strive to shed light on this complex and controversial chapter in history.

The Manhattan Project's Impact on Scientists' Conscience

The development of the atomic bomb during the Manhattan Project had a profound impact on the conscience of the scientists involved. This subchapter delves into the ethical and moral dilemmas faced by these brilliant minds as they grappled with the implications of their groundbreaking scientific discoveries.

At the heart of these dilemmas was the realization that their work could potentially unleash an unprecedented level of destruction. The scientists, including prominent figures like Albert Einstein, found themselves torn between their patriotic duty to contribute to the war effort and their concerns about the devastating consequences of their work.

For many scientists, their involvement in the Manhattan Project led to a crisis of conscience. They were faced with the immense responsibility of creating a weapon capable of ending the war, but also capable of causing unimaginable suffering and loss of life. The knowledge that their discoveries could change the course of history weighed heavily on their minds.

Some scientists, like J. Robert Oppenheimer, the director of the Los Alamos Laboratory, experienced a deep sense of remorse and guilt as they witnessed the devastating power of the atomic bomb. Oppenheimer famously quoted the Bhagavad Gita, saying, "Now I am become Death, the destroyer of worlds." This quote encapsulates the profound impact the project had on the scientists' conscience, as they grappled with the moral implications of their work.

The ethical debates surrounding the Manhattan Project continue to this day. Historians and scholars have questioned whether the use of atomic weapons was necessary to end World War II, and whether alternatives could have been pursued. The long-term effects of the bomb on the environment and human health have also raised important ethical considerations.

Additionally, the Manhattan Project played a pivotal role in shaping post-war international relations. The project's success propelled the United States into a position of scientific and military dominance, setting the stage for the Cold War and the arms race with the Soviet Union.

The legacy of the Manhattan Project is fraught with ongoing debates. Historians continue to grapple with the ethical implications of the project, as well as its impact on the trajectory of scientific research and international relations. Understanding the impact of the project on scientists' conscience is crucial to fully grasp the complexity of this pivotal moment in history.

Balancing Scientific Progress with Humanitarian Concerns

The development of the atomic bomb during the Manhattan Project marked a significant scientific breakthrough that forever changed the course of history. However, this immense achievement also raised profound ethical and humanitarian concerns that continue to be debated to this day. In this subchapter, we delve into the delicate balance between scientific progress and humanitarian considerations that the scientists involved in the Manhattan Project had to grapple with.

The Manhattan Project brought together some of the brightest minds of the time, including renowned scientists like Albert Einstein. These individuals, driven by a desire to push the boundaries of human knowledge, found themselves facing an unprecedented moral dilemma. On one hand, they understood the potential destructive power of the atomic bomb, and the immense suffering it could inflict if used as a weapon of war. On the other hand, they believed that the development of this technology was crucial in order to prevent Nazi Germany from obtaining it first.

The scientists involved in the Manhattan Project were acutely aware of the ethical implications of their work. Many grappled with their conscience and the consequences of their actions. They recognized that the bomb they were creating had the potential to cause immeasurable loss of life, and yet they felt compelled to continue their research in order to protect their own country and the world from the horrors of Nazism.

This ethical dilemma was further complicated by the race between the United States and Nazi Germany to develop atomic weapons. The knowledge that the enemy was also working towards the same goal heightened the urgency among the scientists involved. They faced immense pressure to succeed, knowing that failure could mean catastrophic consequences for their own nation and the world at large.

In their quest for scientific progress, the scientists involved in the Manhattan Project also had to navigate the complexities of espionage and intelligence operations. The project was shrouded in secrecy, with spies from both sides attempting to gather information and sabotage one another's efforts. This added yet another layer of moral ambiguity, as the scientists had to grapple with the question of whether the ends justified the means.

The impact of the atomic bomb on the end of World War II cannot be understated. Its devastating power led to the surrender of Japan and the subsequent conclusion of the war. However, the environmental consequences and long-term effects of the bomb were also significant. The devastating effects of the bombs dropped on Hiroshima and Nagasaki raised concerns about the ethical implications of using such destructive weapons.

The legacy of the Manhattan Project continues to shape discussions on the use of atomic weapons and their place in warfare. The project's influence on the Cold War and the arms race between the United States and the Soviet Union further underscored the complex relationship between scientific progress and humanitarian concerns.

In this subchapter, we explore the ethical and moral dilemmas faced by the scientists involved in the Manhattan Project, the espionage and intelligence operations that surrounded their work, and the long-lasting impact of their scientific breakthrough on international relations, the environment, and ongoing debates surrounding the use of atomic weapons in warfare. By examining the historical context and the perspectives of the scientists themselves, we hope to shed light on the delicate balance between scientific progress and humanitarian concerns that continues to challenge us today.

Reflections on the Decision to Drop the Bomb

The decision to drop the atomic bomb on Hiroshima and Nagasaki in August 1945 remains one of the most controversial and consequential choices in human history. As historians, it is our duty to examine this decision from various angles, considering its scientific, ethical, political, and diplomatic dimensions.

From the scientific perspective, the Manhattan Project represented a remarkable feat of human ingenuity and innovation. The breakthroughs achieved by the project's brilliant scientists, including Albert Einstein, forever transformed our understanding of nuclear physics. They harnessed the immense power locked within the atom, leading to the creation of the atomic bomb. However, this scientific achievement also gave rise to profound moral dilemmas.

The ethical and moral dilemmas faced by the scientists involved in the Manhattan Project were immense. They grappled with the implications of their work, knowing that the destructive potential of the atomic bomb was unparalleled. Oppenheimer, the project's scientific director, famously remarked, "Now I am become Death, the destroyer of worlds." This sentiment reflects the weight of responsibility that hung over the scientists' heads.

Espionage and intelligence operations played a pivotal role in the Manhattan Project. The project was shrouded in secrecy, and both the United States and Nazi Germany engaged in a race to develop atomic weapons. The intelligence efforts surrounding the project were extensive and had a profound impact on the outcome of World War II. The success of the Manhattan Project in creating the atomic bomb gave the United States a decisive advantage, bringing the war to a swift conclusion.

The consequences of dropping the bomb were not limited to the end of the war. The environmental impact and long-term effects of the atomic bomb were substantial. The bombings of Hiroshima and Nagasaki resulted in immense loss of life and widespread devastation. The long-lasting effects of radiation exposure continue to impact the survivors and their descendants to this day.

The political and diplomatic implications of the Manhattan Project were far-reaching. The use of atomic weapons altered the balance of power and ushered in a new era of international relations. The United States emerged as the dominant superpower, and the atomic bomb became a symbol of its military might. This, in turn, set the stage for the Cold War and the arms race between the United States and the Soviet Union.

The legacy of the Manhattan Project remains a subject of ongoing debate. While some argue that the bombings were necessary to end the war and save lives, others question the morality of using such devastating weapons. The decision to drop the bomb continues to raise profound questions about the nature of warfare and the limits of human morality.

In conclusion, reflections on the decision to drop the bomb are complex and multifaceted. As historians, it is our duty to delve into the scientific, ethical, political, and diplomatic aspects surrounding the Manhattan Project. By examining these different angles, we can gain a deeper understanding of this pivotal moment in history and its lasting impact on the world.

Chapter 5: The Espionage and Intelligence Operations Surrounding the Manhattan Project

Soviet Spies and the Manhattan Project

Throughout the history of the Manhattan Project, one of the most significant and intriguing aspects was the presence of Soviet spies within the project. The infiltration of Soviet intelligence into the top-secret program had profound implications for the development of atomic weapons during World War II and the subsequent Cold War.

The Soviet Union, aware of the potential threat posed by the Manhattan Project, spared no effort in gathering intelligence on the project's progress. Soviet spies, such as Klaus Fuchs, Theodore Hall, and David Greenglass, managed to penetrate the project's inner circles, providing the Soviets with crucial information about the development of atomic bombs.

These spies operated covertly, working as scientists and technicians within the project. They were able to access classified information and pass it along to the Soviet Union, significantly accelerating their own atomic weapons program. The information they provided included details about the design of the bomb, the production of fissile materials, and the overall progress of the project.

The impact of these espionage activities was profound. The Soviet Union was able to develop its own atomic bomb much earlier than anticipated, catching the United States by surprise. The successful testing of their first atomic bomb in 1949 marked a significant turning point in the global balance of power and ignited the arms race between the United States and the Soviet Union.

The revelation of Soviet spies within the Manhattan Project had far-reaching consequences for post-war international relations. It led to increased suspicion and mistrust between the United States and the Soviet Union, fueling the tensions that defined the Cold War era. The knowledge that the Soviets had acquired atomic weapons technology through espionage intensified the arms race and created a sense of urgency in the United States to maintain its nuclear superiority.

The legacy of the Soviet spies within the Manhattan Project continues to be a subject of debate and controversy. Some argue that their actions ultimately contributed to the deterrence of nuclear war during the Cold War, while others criticize their betrayal of national secrets. The ethical and moral dilemmas faced by the scientists involved in the Manhattan Project were further complicated by the presence of these spies, adding an additional layer of secrecy and mistrust.

The story of Soviet spies and their infiltration of the Manhattan Project is a fascinating chapter in the history of espionage and intelligence. It highlights the complex and intertwined relationship between scientific discovery, international politics, and the pursuit of national security. Understanding the role of these spies sheds light on the broader context of the Manhattan Project and its enduring impact on the world.

The Venona Project and Decrypting Soviet Espionage

During the height of the Cold War, the United States found itself engaged in a deadly race for global dominance with the Soviet Union. As tensions mounted, both sides sought to gain any advantage they could, including through espionage and intelligence operations. One of the most important initiatives in this covert war was the Venona Project, a top-secret program aimed at decrypting Soviet communications.

The Venona Project was born out of the realization that the Soviet Union had infiltrated numerous espionage networks within the United States.

Suspecting that vital information was being passed to the Soviets, American intelligence agencies embarked on a mission to crack the codes used by their adversaries. This project, which began in the early 1940s, proved to be a pivotal turning point in the intelligence war.

Led by a team of brilliant cryptanalysts, the Venona Project painstakingly decrypted thousands of Soviet messages intercepted by American intelligence agencies. These messages provided unprecedented insights into the activities of Soviet spies in the United States. The decrypted cables revealed the identities of numerous Soviet agents, including those who had penetrated the Manhattan Project, the top-secret program that produced the atomic bomb.

The revelations of the Venona Project had profound implications for the Manhattan Project and the scientists involved. It became clear that Soviet spies had gained access to highly classified information, raising concerns about the security of the project and the potential for Soviet development of atomic weapons. The exposure of these spies also led to a heightened sense of paranoia within the scientific community, as scientists questioned the loyalty of their colleagues.

Furthermore, the Venona Project shed light on the wide-ranging extent of Soviet espionage in the United States. It revealed a vast network of spies, agents, and collaborators operating within the country, posing a significant threat to national security. The decrypted messages provided invaluable intelligence and helped to dismantle Soviet espionage networks, significantly weakening their capabilities.

The legacy of the Venona Project continues to be the subject of ongoing debate and analysis. Historians continue to examine the impact of these decrypted messages on the Cold War, international relations, and the arms race between the United States and the Soviet Union. The project serves as a reminder of the importance of intelligence and the enduring struggle between rival nations for supremacy in the shadows.

In conclusion, the Venona Project played a pivotal role in the intelligence operations surrounding the Manhattan Project and the broader Cold War. Its decryption of Soviet communications exposed the extent of Soviet espionage in the United States, raising concerns about the security of the atomic bomb program. The project's legacy continues to be the subject of historical analysis, highlighting the critical role of intelligence in the complex web of international relations and the ongoing debates surrounding the use of atomic weapons in warfare.

Counterintelligence Efforts and Security Breaches

Counterintelligence efforts played a crucial role in the Manhattan Project, the top-secret program that produced the atomic bomb during World War II. As the project involved groundbreaking scientific discoveries and breakthroughs, it attracted the attention of various foreign intelligence agencies, most notably the Soviet Union. This subchapter delves into the espionage and intelligence operations surrounding the Manhattan Project, shedding light on the security breaches that occurred and the measures taken to mitigate them.

The scientists involved in the Manhattan Project, including prominent figures like Albert Einstein, faced ethical and moral dilemmas. They grappled with the idea of creating a weapon of mass destruction, knowing the devastating consequences it could have on humanity. This internal struggle heightened the need for robust security measures to protect the project from foreign spies and ensure its secrecy.

Despite the utmost precautions taken, security breaches did occur. Soviet intelligence, led by the infamous spy network known as the Cambridge Five, successfully infiltrated the Manhattan Project. These Soviet spies, including Klaus Fuchs and Theodore Hall, obtained classified information about the atomic bomb's development and shared it with the Soviet Union. Their actions not only compromised the project's security but also had far-reaching implications for post-war international relations and the Cold War.

To counter these security breaches, the Manhattan Project implemented extensive counterintelligence efforts. They established a comprehensive system of background checks, security clearances, and compartmentalization to restrict access to sensitive information. This system ensured that only trusted individuals had access to classified data, minimizing the risk of espionage.

Furthermore, the project collaborated closely with the Office of Strategic Services (OSS), the predecessor to the Central Intelligence Agency (CIA). The OSS provided intelligence support and conducted investigations to identify potential security threats. They worked in conjunction with the Federal Bureau of Investigation (FBI) to apprehend Soviet spies operating within the project.

The security breaches and counterintelligence efforts surrounding the Manhattan Project had a profound impact on the development of post-war international relations. The revelation of Soviet espionage not only strained relations between the United States and the Soviet Union but also fueled the arms race between the two superpowers during the Cold War era.

Today, the legacy of the Manhattan Project and its security breaches continue to spark ongoing debates. The ethical implications of developing and using atomic weapons in warfare remain a topic of intense discussion. The lessons learned from the counterintelligence efforts during the project continue to shape intelligence practices and policies in the modern world.

In conclusion, the subchapter on counterintelligence efforts and security breaches highlights the challenges faced by the Manhattan Project in safeguarding its groundbreaking research. It explores the impact of espionage on the project, the measures taken to mitigate security breaches, and the enduring debates surrounding the use of atomic weapons in warfare. By delving into these aspects, historians gain a deeper understanding of the complex dynamics surrounding the Manhattan Project and its far-reaching consequences.

The Legacy of Espionage in the Atomic Age

The Manhattan Project, one of the most significant scientific endeavors of the 20th century, was shrouded in secrecy and intrigue. While the project's primary goal was to develop the atomic bomb during World War II, the espionage and intelligence operations surrounding it left a lasting legacy on the field of intelligence and forever changed the course of history.

The Manhattan Project attracted the attention of various intelligence agencies, both domestic and foreign, who sought to gain insight into the United States' nuclear weapons program. Soviet spies, in particular, were able to infiltrate the project and gather crucial information about the atomic bomb's development. This espionage not only had immediate implications for the war effort but also set the stage for the subsequent Cold War and arms race between the United States and the Soviet Union.

The role of espionage in the Manhattan Project cannot be overstated. It not only highlighted the importance of intelligence gathering and counterintelligence but also raised ethical and moral dilemmas for those involved. Scientists, who were driven by their desire to end the war and protect their country, faced the stark reality that their work could be used for devastating purposes. These individuals grappled with the ethical implications of their actions, knowing that the atomic bomb had the potential to cause immense destruction.

Furthermore, the legacy of espionage in the atomic age has had far-reaching implications for post-war international relations. The Manhattan Project's success marked a significant shift in the balance of power, with the United States emerging as the world's leading nuclear power. This newfound power had political and diplomatic implications, as the United States sought to assert its dominance and influence in the post-war world. The arms race between the United States and the Soviet Union, fueled by the development of atomic weapons, defined much of the Cold War era.

Today, the legacy of the Manhattan Project and the ongoing debates surrounding the use of atomic weapons in warfare continue to shape our understanding of the atomic age. Historians grapple with the ethical and moral dilemmas faced by scientists involved in the project, while also studying the environmental consequences and long-term effects of the atomic bomb's production. The Manhattan Project's influence on the Cold War and the arms race between the United States and the Soviet Union remains a topic of great interest and significance.

In conclusion, the legacy of espionage in the atomic age is a complex and multifaceted topic. It encompasses the intelligence operations surrounding the Manhattan Project, the ethical dilemmas faced by scientists, and the long-term impact on international relations. By examining this legacy, historians gain valuable insights into the scientific discoveries, political implications, and ongoing debates surrounding the use of atomic weapons in warfare. The Manhattan Project's role in shaping the world as we know it today cannot be understated.

Chapter 6: The Impact of the Manhattan Project on the End of World War II

The Manhattan Project's Contribution to Victory

During World War II, the Manhattan Project emerged as one of the most significant scientific endeavors in history, ultimately leading to the development of the atomic bomb. This top-secret program, shrouded in shadows of secrecy, played a pivotal role in the Allied victory and forever changed the course of warfare and international relations.

At its core, the Manhattan Project was a race against time. The United States, driven by the fear that Nazi Germany might develop an atomic weapon first, assembled a team of brilliant scientists and engineers. Led by prominent figures like Albert Einstein, the project harnessed the power of scientific discovery and breakthroughs to unlock the secrets of nuclear fission.

The project's contribution to victory cannot be overstated. The successful development and deployment of the atomic bomb brought an end to the war in the Pacific, saving countless lives that would have been lost in a conventional invasion of Japan. The bombings of Hiroshima and Nagasaki sent a clear message to Japan, leading to their surrender and the eventual end of World War II.

However, the ethical and moral dilemmas faced by the scientists involved cannot be ignored. The destructive power of the atomic bomb raised profound questions about the limits of scientific progress and the responsibility of its creators. These dilemmas continue to fuel ongoing debates surrounding the use of atomic weapons in warfare.

The Manhattan Project also had far-reaching political and diplomatic implications. The United States' possession of atomic weapons solidified its position as a global superpower and reshaped the post-war international order. The project's influence on the Cold War and the subsequent arms race between the United States and the Soviet Union cannot be understated, as it set the stage for decades of tension and competition.

Furthermore, the environmental consequences and long-term effects of the atomic bomb have had lasting impacts. The devastation caused by the bombings of Hiroshima and Nagasaki serves as a haunting reminder of the destructive power that humanity possesses. The legacy of the Manhattan Project continues to shape discussions on nuclear disarmament and non-proliferation.

In conclusion, the Manhattan Project's contribution to victory in World War II cannot be overstated. It not only brought an end to the war but also forever changed the course of history. From the scientific discoveries and breakthroughs to the ethical dilemmas and political implications, the Manhattan Project's influence reverberates to this day. As historians, it is our duty to study and understand the complexities of this top-secret program and its ongoing legacy.

The Role of Atomic Weapons in Japan's Surrender

The surrender of Japan in World War II has been a topic of great historical debate and speculation. One of the key factors that led to Japan's decision to surrender was the use of atomic weapons by the United States. This subchapter delves into the role of atomic weapons in Japan's surrender, shedding light on the complex dynamics and consequences surrounding this historic event.

The Manhattan Project, the top-secret program that produced the atomic bomb, played a pivotal role in the development and utilization of atomic weapons. The scientific discoveries and breakthroughs achieved during the Manhattan Project enabled the creation of devastating and unprecedented weapons of mass destruction.

Prominent scientists, including Albert Einstein, were instrumental in the Manhattan Project. Their expertise and contributions pushed the boundaries of scientific knowledge, leading to the successful development of atomic weapons. However, the ethical and moral dilemmas faced by these scientists cannot be overlooked. The immense destructive power of atomic bombs raised questions about the consequences of their use and the responsibility of scientists involved.

The espionage and intelligence operations surrounding the Manhattan Project added another layer of complexity to the use of atomic weapons. The race between the United States and Nazi Germany to develop atomic weapons intensified the urgency and secrecy surrounding the project. The successful completion of the Manhattan Project gave the United States a significant advantage in the war and influenced post-war international relations.

The impact of the atomic bomb on the end of World War II cannot be underestimated. The bombings of Hiroshima and Nagasaki caused immense devastation and loss of life, forcing Japan to surrender. The decision to employ atomic weapons sparked debates about the necessity and morality of such actions.

The environmental consequences and long-term effects of the atomic bomb produced by the Manhattan Project have persisted to this day. The legacy of nuclear weapons and their potential for catastrophic destruction continues to shape global politics and security.

The use of atomic weapons also had political and diplomatic implications for post-war international relations. The United States' monopoly on atomic weapons during the initial years of the Cold War heightened tensions with the Soviet Union and initiated an arms race that defined the era.

The Manhattan Project's influence on the Cold War and the arms race between the United States and the Soviet Union cannot be overstated. The development and proliferation of nuclear weapons became a central concern of international politics, leading to the establishment of arms control agreements and non-proliferation treaties.

The legacy of the Manhattan Project and the ongoing debates surrounding the use of atomic weapons in warfare continue to shape contemporary discussions. The ethical, moral, and strategic considerations surrounding the use of nuclear weapons remain contentious topics, generating discussions about national security, deterrence, and disarmament.

In conclusion, the role of atomic weapons in Japan's surrender was a defining moment in history. The Manhattan Project and the use of atomic bombs had far-reaching consequences for scientific, political, and ethical realms. Understanding this pivotal event in World War II history is crucial for comprehending the complexities and ongoing debates surrounding the use of atomic weapons in warfare.

Evaluating the Strategic Significance of the Bomb

The development of the atomic bomb during the Manhattan Project brought about a new era in warfare and forever altered the course of history. This subchapter aims to evaluate the strategic significance of this devastating weapon, shedding light on its impact on World War II and the subsequent years that followed.

From a military standpoint, the atomic bomb provided a game-changing advantage to the United States. With its immense destructive power, it offered the potential to swiftly end the war by forcing Japan's surrender. The bombings of Hiroshima and Nagasaki demonstrated the devastating capabilities of this weapon, leading to Japan's capitulation and the cessation of hostilities in the Pacific theater. The strategic significance here cannot be overstated, as it saved countless lives that would have been lost in a protracted invasion of Japan.

Furthermore, the atomic bomb served as a deterrent during the Cold War. The successful development of this weapon by the United States paved the way for the arms race between the U.S. and the Soviet Union. The presence of nuclear weapons on both sides created a balance of terror, preventing direct conflict between the superpowers. It was the fear of mutually assured destruction that kept the Cold War from escalating into a full-scale nuclear war.

However, the strategic significance of the bomb also comes with ethical and moral dilemmas. The immense destruction caused by the bombings of Hiroshima and Nagasaki raised questions about the proportionality of using such a weapon. Historians have debated whether alternatives, such as a demonstration of the bomb's power or a more targeted strike, could have achieved the same outcome without inflicting such devastation on civilian populations.

The strategic significance of the bomb also extends to its impact on post-war international relations. The possession of nuclear weapons became a symbol of power and prestige, leading to an arms race between the U.S. and the Soviet Union. This race for superiority further heightened tensions during the Cold War and shaped the geopolitical landscape for decades to come.

In conclusion, evaluating the strategic significance of the bomb requires an examination of its military, ethical, and diplomatic implications. While it played a decisive role in ending World War II and shaping the Cold War, it also raised significant ethical questions and had far-reaching consequences for international relations. Understanding the complexities of this weapon is essential for historians studying the Manhattan Project and its enduring impact on the world.

Controversies Surrounding the Bombings of Hiroshima and Nagasaki

The bombings of Hiroshima and Nagasaki during World War II remain one of the most controversial events in human history. In this subchapter, we will delve into the numerous debates and controversies surrounding these catastrophic events that forever changed the course of warfare.

The decision to drop atomic bombs on Hiroshima and Nagasaki was rooted in the Manhattan Project, the top-secret program that produced the first atomic bomb. While the bombings undoubtedly hastened the end of the war and saved countless lives, they raised profound ethical and moral dilemmas. Historians have long debated whether the bombings were necessary or if alternative options could have been pursued to achieve a swift Japanese surrender.

Prominent scientists such as Albert Einstein played a crucial role in the Manhattan Project and its scientific discoveries and breakthroughs. However, many scientists involved in the project, including Einstein himself, grappled with the ethical implications of creating such a devastating weapon. The immense power of the atomic bomb brought about a moral crisis that forced scientists to question whether the ends justified the means.

Espionage and intelligence operations also surrounded the Manhattan Project, as the race between the United States and Nazi Germany to develop atomic weapons intensified. The project's secrecy and the efforts to prevent leaks and sabotage have been subjects of extensive research and scrutiny. The discovery of Soviet spies within the project added another layer of controversy and suspicion.

The bombings had far-reaching political and diplomatic implications, shaping post-war international relations. They established the United States as the world's dominant superpower and ushered in the nuclear age. The use of atomic weapons created a delicate balance of power during the Cold War and ignited an arms race between the United States and the Soviet Union.

Moreover, the environmental consequences and long-term effects of the atomic bomb continue to be a topic of concern. The bombings resulted in immense destruction and loss of life, leaving behind devastated landscapes and a legacy of radiation-related illnesses for generations to come.

Today, the legacy of the Manhattan Project and the ongoing debates surrounding the use of atomic weapons in warfare persist. Historians continue to grapple with the ethical implications of the bombings, questioning the moral justifications and exploring alternative scenarios. These controversies highlight the complex nature of scientific advancements, the role of intelligence in war, and the profound impact of technology on humanity.

In conclusion, the controversies surrounding the bombings of Hiroshima and Nagasaki reflect the multifaceted nature of the Manhattan Project. From scientific breakthroughs and moral dilemmas to espionage and political ramifications, these events continue to shape our understanding of World War II and the subsequent global order.

Chapter 7: The Environmental Consequences and Long-Term Effects of the Atomic Bomb Produced by the Manhattan Project

The Devastation of Hiroshima and Nagasaki

The events that unfolded in Hiroshima and Nagasaki in August 1945 remain some of the most controversial and tragic moments in human history. The atomic bombings of these two Japanese cities by the United States marked the culmination of the top-secret Manhattan Project, a program that produced the world's first atomic bomb during World War II. The devastation caused by these bombings forever changed the course of warfare, international relations, and our understanding of the power of science.

The scientific discoveries and breakthroughs achieved by the Manhattan Project were unparalleled. Led by prominent scientists such as J. Robert Oppenheimer and Albert Einstein, the project harnessed the theories of nuclear fission and fusion to create a weapon of unimaginable destruction. The successful test of the bomb in the New Mexico desert in July 1945 paved the way for the fateful decision to use it against Japan.

However, the ethical and moral dilemmas faced by the scientists involved in the Manhattan Project were immense. They grappled with the knowledge that their creation could cause untold civilian casualties. Despite these concerns, the urgency of ending the war and the fear of Nazi Germany developing atomic weapons pushed them to proceed.

The espionage and intelligence operations surrounding the Manhattan Project further added to its secrecy and complexity. Soviet agents infiltrated the project, gathering valuable information that would later aid the Soviet Union in its own pursuit of atomic weapons. This intelligence struggle intensified the political and diplomatic implications of the project for post-war international relations, as it fueled the arms race between the United States and the Soviet Union during the Cold War.

The environmental consequences and long-term effects of the atomic bomb produced by the Manhattan Project were devastating. The immediate impact of the bombings was the loss of over 200,000 lives, with countless others suffering from radiation sickness and long-term health effects. The long-lasting environmental damage and the psychological scars left on survivors continue to be felt to this day.

The legacy of the Manhattan Project and the use of atomic weapons in warfare remains a topic of ongoing debate. Historians continue to grapple with the question of whether the bombings were necessary to end the war quickly or if alternative options could have been pursued. The race between the United States and Nazi Germany to develop atomic weapons further underscores the global implications of the project and the urgency felt by the Allies.

In conclusion, the devastation of Hiroshima and Nagasaki represents a turning point in human history. The Manhattan Project's scientific achievements, the moral dilemmas faced by its scientists, the espionage surrounding it, and the far-reaching consequences of the atomic bomb all contribute to its significance. Understanding and reflecting upon this chapter of history is crucial for historians and anyone interested in the complex interplay between science, ethics, and warfare.

Radiation Effects and Long-Term Health Consequences

The development and use of atomic bombs during World War II, as part of the Manhattan Project, brought about a significant scientific breakthrough that forever changed the course of history. However, the consequences of this powerful weapon extend far beyond the immediate destruction and devastation caused by its detonation.

Radiation effects and long-term health consequences have been topics of concern and debate ever since the atomic bomb was first used. The immense release of energy during the explosion resulted in the dispersal of radioactive materials into the surrounding environment. These materials, such as uranium and plutonium, can have severe and lasting effects on human health.

One of the primary health concerns associated with radiation exposure is the development of various forms of cancer. Studies have shown that individuals exposed to high levels of radiation, whether through the initial blast or subsequent fallout, have an increased risk of developing leukemia, thyroid cancer, and other malignancies. The effects of radiation can be particularly devastating for children and unborn babies, as their rapidly dividing cells are more vulnerable to damage.

Apart from cancer, radiation exposure can also lead to other long-term health issues. Genetic mutations, birth defects, and reproductive problems have all been documented among survivors and their descendants. These health consequences extend beyond the immediate survivors and can impact future generations, leading to ongoing concerns about the legacy of the atomic bomb.

The environmental consequences of the atomic bomb are equally significant. The explosion and subsequent fallout from the bomb resulted in widespread contamination of the surrounding areas. Soil, water, and air were all contaminated with radioactive materials, posing a risk to both human and animal populations. The long-lasting effects of this contamination are still being felt today, with ongoing efforts to mitigate the environmental impact.

The study of radiation effects and long-term health consequences has played a crucial role in shaping international discussions and policies surrounding nuclear weapons. The devastating impact of the atomic bomb served as a stark reminder of the destructive potential of these weapons and prompted efforts to prevent their use in warfare.

Understanding the long-term health consequences of radiation exposure is not only important for historical purposes but also for informing current debates surrounding nuclear weapons and their potential use. By examining the legacy of the Manhattan Project, historians can shed light on the ethical, moral, and environmental implications of nuclear weapons, thereby contributing to ongoing discussions about disarmament, non-proliferation, and the pursuit of peaceful alternatives.

In conclusion, the radiation effects and long-term health consequences of the atomic bomb developed during the Manhattan Project have had a profound and lasting impact. By examining the scientific, ethical, and environmental dimensions of these consequences, historians can provide valuable insights into the legacy of the Manhattan Project and contribute to ongoing debates surrounding nuclear weapons and their implications for global security.

Environmental Contamination and Cleanup Efforts

The Manhattan Project, one of the most secretive and significant scientific endeavors of the 20th century, not only revolutionized the world of atomic science but also had far-reaching environmental consequences. As historians delve into the depths of this top-secret program, it becomes apparent that the environmental contamination resulting from the production of atomic bombs was a significant concern that lingered long after the project's conclusion.

The scientific breakthroughs achieved during the Manhattan Project were monumental, but they came at a great cost to the environment.

The large-scale production of enriched uranium and plutonium required immense amounts of energy, resulting in the release of hazardous byproducts and radioactive waste into the surrounding areas. The extraction and processing of uranium ore, for example, left behind contaminated soil and water sources, posing a serious threat to both human health and the ecosystem.

Cleanup efforts were undertaken in the years following the Manhattan Project's completion to address the environmental contamination caused by the production of atomic bombs. These efforts focused on decontaminating sites, such as Oak Ridge, Hanford, and Los Alamos, where the majority of the research and production facilities were located. Specialized teams were tasked with the challenging job of removing radioactive materials, dismantling contaminated structures, and treating contaminated soil and water.

However, the environmental consequences of the atomic bomb were not limited to the production sites alone. The bombings of Hiroshima and Nagasaki resulted in widespread devastation, causing extensive damage to the environment. The immediate impact included fires, destruction of buildings and vegetation, and the contamination of air, water, and soil with radioactive particles. The long-term effects of radiation exposure on the survivors, known as hibakusha, and the environment have been a subject of ongoing study and concern.

The legacy of the Manhattan Project's environmental contamination and cleanup efforts is still felt today. The need for ongoing monitoring and remediation remains, as the radioactive waste generated during the project's heyday has a long half-life and poses a persistent threat to human health and the environment. The lessons learned from the environmental consequences of the atomic bomb have also shaped subsequent discussions and policies regarding the use of nuclear energy and weapons.

As historians explore the intricacies of the Manhattan Project, it is crucial to shine a light on the environmental impact and cleanup efforts that followed in its wake. Understanding the historical context and long-term consequences of this top-secret program allows for a comprehensive examination of the ethical, scientific, and geopolitical dimensions surrounding the development and use of atomic weapons. By considering the environmental legacy of the Manhattan Project, historians can contribute to ongoing debates about the responsible use of nuclear technology and its implications for future generations.

Lessons Learned for Nuclear Weapons Testing

The subchapter titled "Lessons Learned for Nuclear Weapons Testing" aims to provide historians with valuable insights into the Manhattan Project's nuclear weapons testing and the subsequent implications for the development and use of atomic weapons in warfare. This chapter delves into the key lessons that emerged from the project and how they continue to shape our understanding of nuclear weapons today.

One crucial lesson learned from the Manhattan Project's nuclear weapons testing was the immense destructive power of atomic bombs. Scientists involved in the project witnessed firsthand the devastating effects of the bombs on the cities of Hiroshima and Nagasaki, leading to an estimated 200,000 deaths. This realization underscored the urgent need for international cooperation and the establishment of arms control agreements to prevent the use of nuclear weapons in the future.

Another significant lesson was the importance of ethical considerations in scientific research and development. The scientists involved in the Manhattan Project grappled with profound moral dilemmas regarding the use of atomic bombs. The immense loss of life and the long-term environmental consequences raised questions about the ethical implications of their work. This chapter explores the debates that ensued and the impact these ethical dilemmas had on post-war international relations.

Furthermore, the chapter discusses the role of espionage and intelligence operations in the Manhattan Project. The project was shrouded in secrecy, and the United States went to great lengths to prevent Nazi Germany from acquiring nuclear weapons. The successful espionage efforts of the Allies, such as Operation Alsos, provided critical intelligence that contributed to the eventual defeat of Germany. These intelligence operations highlight the importance of intelligence gathering and counterintelligence measures in nuclear weapons development.

The subchapter also touches upon the political and diplomatic implications of the Manhattan Project. The successful development of atomic bombs by the United States dramatically shifted the balance of power in the post-war world, leading to the start of the Cold War and the arms race between the United States and the Soviet Union. Understanding the political and diplomatic consequences of the Manhattan Project is crucial for comprehending the tensions that defined international relations during the Cold War era.

In conclusion, the subchapter "Lessons Learned for Nuclear Weapons Testing" offers historians a comprehensive analysis of the Manhattan Project's impact on the development and use of atomic weapons. It explores key insights gained from the project, including the destructive power of nuclear weapons, the ethical considerations surrounding their use, the role of espionage, and the political and diplomatic implications. By understanding these lessons, we can continue to engage in meaningful discussions about the legacy and ongoing debates surrounding the Manhattan Project and the use of atomic weapons in warfare.

Chapter 8: The Race Between the United States and Nazi Germany to Develop Atomic Weapons During World War II

Germany's Failed Efforts in Nuclear Research

During World War II, the Manhattan Project emerged as a top-secret program that successfully produced the atomic bomb. However, little is known about Germany's own efforts in nuclear research, which ultimately failed to achieve the same groundbreaking results. This subchapter delves into the reasons behind Germany's unsuccessful endeavors, shedding light on the scientific, political, and espionage factors that contributed to this outcome.

One key factor in Germany's failure was the lack of collaboration among its scientists. While the Manhattan Project brought together some of the brightest minds in physics, chemistry, and engineering, Germany struggled to establish a cohesive research program. Unlike the United States, where prominent scientists like Albert Einstein played an active role, Germany failed to harness the potential of its scientific community due to internal divisions and rivalries.

Furthermore, Germany faced significant challenges in obtaining the necessary resources and infrastructure for its nuclear research. The country was already stretched thin with wartime demands, and the resources required for a successful nuclear program were simply not available. This limited Germany's ability to conduct large-scale experiments and hindered progress in critical areas such as uranium enrichment and reactor design.

Espionage and intelligence operations also played a role in Germany's failure. The Manhattan Project benefited greatly from the recruitment of talented scientists and the acquisition of critical information through espionage. In contrast, Germany's intelligence efforts were largely ineffective, failing to infiltrate the United States' research facilities or obtain valuable scientific knowledge.

Moreover, Germany's political and diplomatic landscape posed significant challenges. The Nazi regime, despite its fervent pursuit of scientific advancements, adopted a fierce anti-Semitic ideology that led to the suppression and expulsion of many Jewish scientists. This loss of talent further hampered Germany's efforts to compete with the Manhattan Project.

In the aftermath of World War II, the failure of Germany's nuclear research had profound implications for international relations. The United States' successful development of atomic weapons solidified its position as a global superpower, while Germany's inability to do the same relegated it to a defeated nation.

The legacy of Germany's failed nuclear research continues to spark ongoing debates. Scholars and historians continue to explore the reasons behind Germany's shortcomings, examining the ethical and moral dilemmas faced by its scientists, and considering the environmental consequences and long-term effects of the atomic bomb produced by the Manhattan Project.

In conclusion, Germany's failed efforts in nuclear research during World War II can be attributed to a combination of factors including internal divisions among scientists, resource limitations, ineffective espionage operations, and the political and diplomatic challenges faced by the Nazi regime. Understanding Germany's shortcomings provides valuable insights into the complex history of the Manhattan Project and its enduring legacy in scientific, political, and ethical realms.

Allied Efforts to Prevent Germany from Obtaining the Bomb

During World War II, one of the most critical concerns for the Allied powers was preventing Germany from obtaining the atomic bomb. The potential devastation that this weapon could unleash upon the world was unimaginable, and it was vital to maintain a strategic advantage in the arms race. This subchapter explores the various methods employed by the Allies to hinder Germany's progress in developing atomic weapons.

At the forefront of these efforts was the Manhattan Project itself. This top-secret program, led by some of the world's most brilliant scientists, aimed to develop atomic weapons for the United States. Recognizing the urgency, scientists and researchers from various countries, including displaced Jewish scientists fleeing Nazi persecution, joined forces to prevent the Nazis from harnessing the atom's power.

Intelligence agencies played a crucial role in gathering information about Germany's progress. Spy networks were established in Europe to infiltrate German scientific institutions and gather crucial data. Agents risked their lives to smuggle out information regarding Germany's atomic research and sabotage their efforts wherever possible.

One of the most notable espionage operations was the Alsos Mission. Led by Colonel Boris Pash, this covert unit was tasked with capturing German scientists, securing research materials, and assessing the progress of Germany's atomic program. Their efforts proved fruitful, as they successfully apprehended key German scientists and confiscated vital documents, preventing valuable knowledge from falling into enemy hands.

Simultaneously, the Allies implemented economic sanctions to limit Germany's access to critical resources necessary for atomic research. Supplies of uranium, heavy water, and other essential materials were targeted, causing significant setbacks for the German program. These efforts disrupted Germany's ability to maintain a sustainable atomic research infrastructure.

The Allies also sought to counter Germany's scientific brain drain. Prominent scientists, such as Albert Einstein, who had fled Germany, were actively involved in the Manhattan Project. Their expertise and insights were invaluable in advancing the Allies' own atomic research while simultaneously depriving Germany of their knowledge.

Ultimately, the combined efforts of intelligence operations, economic sanctions, and scientific collaboration proved successful. Germany's atomic program was hampered, and their dreams of obtaining the bomb were never realized. The Manhattan Project's success in developing atomic weapons before Germany ensured that the Allies held a decisive advantage in the war and shaped the course of history.

The Allied efforts to prevent Germany from obtaining the bomb exemplify the complex and multifaceted nature of the Manhattan Project. It highlights the ethical and moral dilemmas faced by scientists involved, the espionage and intelligence operations surrounding the project, and the impact of the project on the end of World War II and post-war international relations. The legacy of the Manhattan Project continues to spark ongoing debates about the use of atomic weapons in warfare and remains a significant influence on the Cold War and the arms race between the United States and the Soviet Union.

The Significance of the United States' Success

The United States' success in the Manhattan Project holds immense significance in various aspects, making it a pivotal event in both scientific and historical realms. The project's accomplishments had a profound impact on the outcome of World War II, the subsequent Cold War, and the development of international relations.

First and foremost, the United States' success in the Manhattan Project resulted in the production of the atomic bomb, a weapon of unprecedented destructive power. This breakthrough in scientific discovery and technological innovation forever changed the course of warfare. The atomic bomb played a crucial role in bringing an end to World War II, as it forced Japan's surrender after the bombings of Hiroshima and Nagasaki. This marked the first and only time atomic weapons were used in warfare, highlighting the immense influence of the Manhattan Project on the outcome of the war.

Furthermore, the success of the Manhattan Project solidified the United States' position as a global superpower. The development and utilization of atomic weapons placed the country at the forefront of military technology, giving it a significant advantage over other nations. This newfound power had far-reaching political and diplomatic implications, shaping post-war international relations. The United States emerged as the dominant force in the world, leading to the formation of alliances, such as NATO, and the subsequent arms race with the Soviet Union during the Cold War.

The success of the Manhattan Project also sparked widespread ethical and moral dilemmas. The scientists involved in the project faced the profound question of whether the use of atomic weapons was justified, considering their devastating consequences. This debate continues to this day, with ongoing discussions about the legacy and implications of the Manhattan Project and the use of atomic weapons in warfare.

Additionally, the environmental consequences and long-term effects of the atomic bomb produced by the Manhattan Project cannot be ignored. The bombings of Hiroshima and Nagasaki caused immense human suffering and left a lasting impact on the environment. The project's success raised concerns about the potential destruction and devastation that nuclear weapons could inflict on the world.

In conclusion, the significance of the United States' success in the Manhattan Project cannot be understated. Its impact on World War II, international relations, the Cold War, and scientific and ethical debates has shaped the course of history. Understanding the achievements and consequences of the project is crucial for historians and those interested in the complex interplay between science, warfare, and global politics.

Implications for the Post-War World Order

The conclusion of World War II marked a significant turning point in global history, with the Manhattan Project playing a pivotal role in shaping the post-war world order. The development and deployment of atomic bombs by the United States had profound implications for international relations, politics, and the balance of power. This subchapter will explore the far-reaching consequences of the Manhattan Project for the post-war era, examining the political, diplomatic, and ethical dimensions of this monumental scientific achievement.

The Manhattan Project's successful production of atomic weapons undoubtedly led to the United States emerging as a dominant global power. The sheer destructive power of the atomic bomb, demonstrated in the bombings of Hiroshima and Nagasaki, established the United States as the preeminent military force. This newfound superiority greatly influenced the geopolitical landscape and set the stage for the ensuing Cold War between the United States and the Soviet Union.

The political and diplomatic implications of the Manhattan Project were vast. The project's success significantly influenced the United States' approach to international relations. The use of atomic bombs raised ethical and moral questions, sparking debates about the necessity of such destructive weapons and the consequences of their use. The bombings of Hiroshima and Nagasaki forever changed the calculus of warfare and forced nations to reassess their military strategies.

Furthermore, the Manhattan Project's influence extended beyond immediate post-war politics. The arms race between the United States and the Soviet Union, fueled by the fear of mutually assured destruction, dominated the latter half of the 20th century. The development of nuclear weapons became a defining feature of this era, with both superpowers accumulating vast arsenals that threatened global stability.

The legacy of the Manhattan Project and its implications continue to shape ongoing debates. The use of atomic weapons in warfare remains a contentious issue, with questions of morality and responsibility still unresolved. Environmental consequences and long-term effects, such as radiation poisoning and the potential for nuclear accidents, raise concerns about the sustainability and safety of nuclear energy.

In conclusion, the Manhattan Project had profound implications for the post-war world order. Its impact on politics, diplomacy, and the balance of power was far-reaching. The development and use of atomic weapons transformed the global landscape and led to an enduring arms race. The legacy of the Manhattan Project and the ongoing debates surrounding its consequences continue to shape international relations and the discourse on the use of atomic weapons in warfare.

Chapter 9: The Political and Diplomatic Implications of the Manhattan Project for Post-War International Relations

The Emergence of the United States as a Superpower

The Manhattan Project was a top-secret program that forever changed the course of history. Through scientific discoveries and breakthroughs, the project produced the most destructive weapon ever created – the atomic bomb. This subchapter explores the emergence of the United States as a superpower as a direct result of the Manhattan Project.

Led by some of the brightest scientific minds of the time, including Albert Einstein, the Manhattan Project pushed the boundaries of human knowledge and technological capabilities. These prominent scientists played a pivotal role in the project, utilizing their expertise to develop the atomic bomb. Their contributions were vital in harnessing the power of nuclear fission and ultimately creating a weapon of immense destruction.

However, the scientists involved in the Manhattan Project also faced profound ethical and moral dilemmas. They grappled with the realization that their scientific breakthroughs could be used to cause unprecedented devastation. This internal struggle added a complex layer to their work, as they were torn between their duty to their country and their personal beliefs.

The Manhattan Project was not without its share of espionage and intelligence operations. Both the United States and Nazi Germany were racing to develop atomic weapons during World War II. The project was shrouded in secrecy, with spies on both sides attempting to gather intelligence and gain an advantage. The intense competition and high stakes added an element of intrigue and danger to the story of the Manhattan Project.

The impact of the Manhattan Project on the end of World War II cannot be overstated. With the successful testing of the atomic bomb, the United States had a decisive advantage over its enemies. The bombings of Hiroshima and Nagasaki brought about the surrender of Japan and effectively ended the war. This unprecedented display of power solidified the United States as a superpower on the world stage.

The political and diplomatic implications of the Manhattan Project extended far beyond the end of World War II. The project had a profound impact on post-war international relations, as the United States emerged as the dominant force. It also set the stage for the Cold War and the subsequent arms race between the United States and the Soviet Union.

The legacy of the Manhattan Project continues to be a subject of ongoing debate. The ethical considerations surrounding the use of atomic weapons in warfare remain highly contested. The environmental consequences and long-term effects of the atomic bomb have also raised concerns. As historians, it is our duty to examine this complex history and engage in critical discussions surrounding the Manhattan Project and its lasting impact on the world.

Nuclear Weapons and the Balance of Power

In the subchapter "Nuclear Weapons and the Balance of Power," we delve into the profound impact of the Manhattan Project on the delicate equilibrium of global power dynamics. This chapter explores how the development and deployment of atomic weapons transformed the geopolitical landscape, shaping the course of history in the aftermath of World War II.

The Manhattan Project, a top-secret program that produced the atomic bomb, introduced a game-changing weapon with unprecedented destructive capabilities. This scientific breakthrough had far-reaching consequences for international relations, sparking a race for nuclear dominance between the United States and Nazi Germany. The project's success hinged on the collaboration of prominent scientists, including the iconic Albert Einstein, whose contributions played a pivotal role in harnessing nuclear energy.

However, the Manhattan Project also raised profound ethical and moral dilemmas for the scientists involved. They grappled with the devastating potential of their creation and the ethical implications of its use in warfare. The book explores the inner conflicts faced by these scientists, shedding light on their motivations, doubts, and the complex decisions they made.

Espionage and intelligence operations surrounding the Manhattan Project further heighten the intrigue surrounding this clandestine endeavor. The book uncovers the stories of espionage agents who sought to infiltrate the project, highlighting the high-stakes covert operations that unfolded during this critical period.

The ultimate impact of the Manhattan Project was felt on the world stage, as the atomic bomb played a decisive role in ending World War II. This chapter explores the historical significance of the bombings of Hiroshima and Nagasaki, examining the immediate and long-term consequences of these devastating attacks.

Moreover, the legacy of the Manhattan Project reverberated long after the war's end. The project's influence on the Cold War and the subsequent arms race between the United States and the Soviet Union is thoroughly examined. The book delves into the political and diplomatic implications of the Manhattan Project, shaping post-war international relations and escalating tensions between the superpowers.

Finally, the subchapter delves into the ongoing debates surrounding the use of atomic weapons in warfare. It explores the ethical, environmental, and long-term consequences of the atomic bomb, providing historians with a comprehensive understanding of the Manhattan Project's legacy and its enduring impact on global society.

Overall, "Nuclear Weapons and the Balance of Power" offers a captivating exploration of the Manhattan Project, shedding light on the scientific discoveries, espionage operations, ethical dilemmas, and geopolitical ramifications that continue to shape our world today.

Cold War Tensions and the Nuclear Arms Race

The subchapter titled "Cold War Tensions and the Nuclear Arms Race" explores the profound influence of the Manhattan Project on the development of the Cold War and the subsequent nuclear arms race between the United States and the Soviet Union. This section delves into the historical context, key events, and the lasting impact of this pivotal period in world history.

Following the end of World War II, tensions between the United States and the Soviet Union began to escalate rapidly. The atomic bomb, a product of the Manhattan Project, played a central role in exacerbating these tensions. The successful testing of the first atomic bomb, codenamed Trinity, in July 1945 marked a turning point in global politics. The United States had demonstrated its immense power and technological superiority, and this knowledge quickly reverberated around the world.

The subchapter explores how the atomic bomb shifted the balance of power and ignited a dangerous competition between the United States and the Soviet Union. The arms race that ensued was characterized by a frantic race to develop more powerful and destructive weapons. Both nations sought to outdo each other, leading to an unprecedented buildup of nuclear arsenals and a constant state of alert.

This subchapter also delves into the political and diplomatic implications of the Manhattan Project for post-war international relations. The United States, aware of its atomic monopoly, used its newfound power to assert dominance and influence global affairs. The Soviet Union, feeling threatened, embarked on its own nuclear program, leading to a dangerous standoff between two superpowers.

The legacy and ongoing debates surrounding the Manhattan Project and the use of atomic weapons in warfare are also explored. Historians continue to grapple with the ethical and moral dilemmas faced by scientists involved in the project. Questions about the long-term environmental consequences and the devastating impact of nuclear weapons on civilian populations remain at the forefront of discussions.

In conclusion, the subchapter "Cold War Tensions and the Nuclear Arms Race" examines the profound impact of the Manhattan Project on the development of the Cold War and the subsequent nuclear arms race. It provides a comprehensive understanding of the historical context, key events, and lasting implications of this critical period in world history. Historians, as well as enthusiasts of the Manhattan Project and its aftermath, will find this subchapter a valuable resource for understanding the complex dynamics that shaped the post-war world.

The Proliferation of Nuclear Technology

The development of nuclear technology during the Manhattan Project had far-reaching implications that extended beyond the end of World War II. This subchapter explores the proliferation of nuclear technology and its impact on various aspects of history, including post-war international relations, the Cold War, and ongoing debates surrounding the use of atomic weapons in warfare.

Following the successful creation of the atomic bomb by the Manhattan Project, the United States found itself in possession of a powerful weapon that would forever change the course of history. The scientific discoveries and breakthroughs achieved during the project paved the way for the rapid development and spread of nuclear technology worldwide.

The role of Albert Einstein and other prominent scientists cannot be underestimated in this process. Their involvement in the Manhattan Project brought attention to the immense destructive power of atomic weapons, leading to ethical and moral dilemmas for the scientists involved. The decision to use these weapons on Hiroshima and Nagasaki raised questions about the ethics of using such devastating force against civilian populations.

The espionage and intelligence operations surrounding the Manhattan Project added another layer of complexity to the proliferation of nuclear technology. The race between the United States and Nazi Germany to develop atomic weapons during World War II highlighted the importance of intelligence gathering and counterintelligence efforts. The race was ultimately won by the United States, which had significant implications for the outcome of the war.

The impact of the Manhattan Project on the end of World War II cannot be overstated. The bombings of Hiroshima and Nagasaki forced Japan's surrender and brought an end to the war in the Pacific. However, the environmental consequences and long-term effects of the atomic bomb were severe. The devastation caused by the bombings raised awareness about the devastating power of nuclear weapons and led to the formation of the United Nations and efforts to prevent the proliferation of these weapons.

The political and diplomatic implications of the Manhattan Project for post-war international relations were significant. The United States emerged as a dominant superpower, and the atomic bomb became a symbol of its military strength. The fear of a nuclear arms race between the United States and the Soviet Union during the Cold War led to the development of nuclear deterrence strategies and the ongoing arms race between the two nations.

The legacy of the Manhattan Project and the ongoing debates surrounding the use of atomic weapons in warfare continue to shape the world today. The ethical considerations, environmental consequences, and potential for catastrophic destruction have led to efforts to control and limit the spread of nuclear technology through international treaties and non-proliferation agreements.

In conclusion, the proliferation of nuclear technology that emerged from the Manhattan Project had profound historical implications. From the scientific breakthroughs to the ethical dilemmas faced by scientists, from the espionage operations to the political and diplomatic implications, the development and use of atomic weapons continue to shape our world. Understanding the legacy of the Manhattan Project and the ongoing debates surrounding nuclear technology is essential for historians and anyone interested in the history of the atomic age.

Chapter 10: The Manhattan Project's Influence on the Cold War and the Arms Race Between the United States and the Soviet Union

The Soviet Union's Acquisition of Atomic Weapons

In the subchapter titled "The Soviet Union's Acquisition of Atomic Weapons" in the book "Shadows of Secrecy: Espionage and Intelligence in the Manhattan Project," we delve into the fascinating story of how the Soviet Union managed to acquire atomic weapons. This section is specifically targeted towards historians and individuals interested in the various aspects of the Manhattan Project.

The race to develop atomic weapons during World War II was not solely between the United States and Nazi Germany. The Soviet Union, under the leadership of Joseph Stalin, also sought to obtain this powerful technology. However, unlike the United States, the Soviet Union did not possess the scientific and industrial infrastructure to develop atomic weapons on its own.

The subchapter explores the espionage and intelligence operations that the Soviet Union engaged in to bridge this gap. Soviet spies, such as Klaus Fuchs and Theodore Hall, infiltrated the Manhattan Project and provided crucial information to the Soviet Union. These individuals played a significant role in expediting the Soviet Union's atomic bomb program.

Furthermore, the subchapter delves into the political and diplomatic implications of the Manhattan Project for post-war international relations. The fact that the Soviet Union successfully acquired atomic weapons significantly altered the balance of power in the world. It led to the beginning of the Cold War and the arms race between the United States and the Soviet Union.

The impact of the Soviet Union's acquisition of atomic weapons on the Cold War and subsequent arms race is also discussed. The knowledge that both superpowers possessed this destructive capability heightened tensions and led to an intense competition to develop more advanced nuclear technology.

Finally, the subchapter touches upon the legacy and ongoing debates surrounding the Manhattan Project and the use of atomic weapons in warfare. The acquisition of atomic weapons by the Soviet Union raised questions about the ethics and morality of their use. It also sparked discussions about the need for international treaties and agreements to prevent the proliferation of nuclear weapons.

Overall, this subchapter sheds light on an often-overlooked aspect of the Manhattan Project – the Soviet Union's acquisition of atomic weapons. It explores the espionage and intelligence operations, the political implications, and the lasting effects on post-war international relations. Historians and those interested in the Manhattan Project will find this section a valuable addition to their understanding of this pivotal moment in history.

Strategic Arms Limitation Talks (SALT) and Arms Control Efforts

The development of atomic weapons during World War II by the Manhattan Project had a profound impact on international relations and the subsequent arms race between the United States and the Soviet Union during the Cold War. In the wake of the devastation caused by the atomic bombings of Hiroshima and Nagasaki, there was a growing recognition of the need for arms control measures to prevent the use of these weapons in future conflicts.

The Strategic Arms Limitation Talks (SALT) were a series of negotiations between the United States and the Soviet Union aimed at limiting the proliferation of nuclear weapons. The talks began in the late 1960s and culminated in the signing of several landmark treaties in the 1970s. The SALT agreements placed restrictions on the number of strategic nuclear weapons that each side could possess and established mechanisms for verifying compliance.

One of the key objectives of the SALT negotiations was to prevent an arms race from spiraling out of control. Both the United States and the Soviet Union recognized the dangers of an unchecked nuclear arms buildup and the potential for a catastrophic conflict. Through SALT, the two superpowers sought to create a stable and predictable nuclear balance that would reduce the risk of miscalculation and escalation.

Arms control efforts, including the SALT negotiations, also had broader political and diplomatic implications. They provided a platform for dialogue and engagement between the United States and the Soviet Union at a time when tensions between the two superpowers were at their peak. By working towards common goals in the area of arms control, the United States and the Soviet Union were able to build trust and establish channels of communication that were crucial for managing the broader dynamics of the Cold War.

While the SALT agreements represented an important step towards arms control, they were not without their limitations and criticisms. Some historians argue that the agreements did not go far enough in limiting nuclear weapons, particularly in the area of tactical or non-strategic weapons. Others contend that the verification mechanisms established by the agreements were flawed and could be easily circumvented.

Nevertheless, the SALT negotiations and subsequent arms control efforts marked a significant departure from the arms race mentality that characterized the early years of the Cold War. They reflected a growing recognition of the need to manage and control the destructive power of nuclear weapons in order to prevent their use in warfare. The legacy of these efforts continues to shape the debate surrounding nuclear disarmament and non-proliferation today.

Mutual Assured Destruction (MAD) and Deterrence

In the realm of international relations and the development of nuclear weapons, the concept of Mutual Assured Destruction (MAD) and deterrence played a significant role during the Manhattan Project. As historians delve into the depths of this top-secret program, it becomes evident that MAD and deterrence were crucial elements that influenced the decisions made by the scientists and policymakers involved.

MAD refers to the doctrine that emerged during the Cold War era, which posited that if two nuclear-armed nations engaged in a conflict, the outcome would result in both parties suffering catastrophic damage. This understanding formed the basis of deterrence, which sought to prevent nuclear war by ensuring that the consequences of such a conflict would be too severe for any rational actor to initiate.

Within the context of the Manhattan Project, MAD and deterrence were central to the ethical and moral dilemmas faced by the scientists. While their scientific discoveries and breakthroughs were groundbreaking, they also carried immense destructive power. The realization that the atomic bomb could cause immense devastation raised questions about the ethical implications of its use.

Additionally, the espionage and intelligence operations surrounding the Manhattan Project were influenced by the concept of deterrence. The United States, aware of the potential for Nazi Germany to develop atomic weapons, sought to maintain a technological advantage to deter any aggressive action. The race between the United States and Nazi

Germany to develop atomic weapons during World War II was, in essence, a race for deterrence.

The impact of the Manhattan Project on the end of World War II cannot be understated. The use of atomic bombs on Hiroshima and Nagasaki led to Japan's surrender, marking a turning point in the conflict. The political and diplomatic implications of the Manhattan Project for post-war international relations were profound, as the United States emerged as the dominant nuclear power, shaping the global balance of power for years to come.

Furthermore, the legacy and ongoing debates surrounding the Manhattan Project and the use of atomic weapons in warfare are deeply intertwined with the concept of MAD and deterrence. Scholars continue to grapple with the ethical considerations of nuclear weapons, the environmental consequences, and the long-term effects of their use.

In conclusion, the subchapter on Mutual Assured Destruction (MAD) and deterrence in "Shadows of Secrecy: Espionage and Intelligence in the Manhattan Project" provides historians with an in-depth exploration of the role these concepts played in the development and use of atomic weapons. From the ethical dilemmas faced by scientists to the political and diplomatic implications, MAD and deterrence shaped the trajectory of the Manhattan Project and its aftermath, leaving a lasting impact on international relations and ongoing debates about the use of atomic weapons.

The End of the Cold War and the Legacy of the Manhattan Project

The end of the Cold War marked a significant turning point in global history, and the legacy of the Manhattan Project played a crucial role in shaping this new era. The project, a top-secret program that produced the atomic bomb during World War II, had far-reaching scientific, political, and ethical implications that reverberated long after the war ended.

Scientifically, the Manhattan Project represented a watershed moment in human understanding of nuclear physics and the potential harnessing of atomic energy. The project's breakthrough discoveries, led by prominent scientists such as Albert Einstein, forever changed the course of scientific research and technology. The unprecedented collaboration between scientists from various disciplines laid the foundation for future advancements in nuclear energy and weaponry, as well as other scientific fields.

However, the ethical and moral dilemmas faced by the scientists involved in the Manhattan Project cannot be overlooked. The decision to create and use the atomic bomb raised profound questions about the responsibility of scientists and the consequences of their actions. The devastating impact of the bombings of Hiroshima and Nagasaki, coupled with the ongoing debates surrounding the use of atomic weapons in warfare, continue to shape discussions on the ethics of scientific research and the limits of technological advancement.

Furthermore, the espionage and intelligence operations surrounding the Manhattan Project added another layer of complexity to its legacy. The race between the United States and Nazi Germany to develop atomic weapons during World War II was a critical aspect of the project's history. The successful efforts to prevent German acquisition of atomic weapons demonstrated the vital role of intelligence and covert operations in shaping global events.

The political and diplomatic implications of the Manhattan Project were far-reaching, both during and after World War II. The project's success solidified the United States' position as a world superpower and played a pivotal role in post-war international relations. The project's influence on the Cold War and the subsequent arms race between the United States and the Soviet Union cannot be underestimated.

The environmental consequences and long-term effects of the atomic bomb produced by the Manhattan Project also demand attention. The devastating power of nuclear weapons became evident, leading to concerns about the long-term effects on human health and the environment. The ongoing debates and regulations surrounding nuclear energy and weapons continue to be shaped by the legacy of the Manhattan Project.

In conclusion, the end of the Cold War marked a pivotal moment in history, and the legacy of the Manhattan Project played a significant role in shaping this new era. The scientific breakthroughs, ethical dilemmas, espionage operations, political implications, and environmental consequences of the project continue to be subjects of study and debate among historians. The Manhattan Project's influence on the world remains profound, and its ongoing legacy continues to spark discussions about the use and control of nuclear weapons in warfare and the ethical responsibilities of scientists.

Chapter 11: The Legacy and Ongoing Debates Surrounding the Manhattan Project and the Use of Atomic Weapons in Warfare

The Moral and Ethical Implications of Nuclear Weapons

In the subchapter titled "The Moral and Ethical Implications of Nuclear Weapons" from the book "Shadows of Secrecy: Espionage and Intelligence in the Manhattan Project," we delve into the profound questions surrounding the development and use of atomic bombs during World War II. This subchapter aims to provide a comprehensive analysis of the moral and ethical dilemmas faced by scientists involved in the Manhattan Project, the consequences of the atomic bomb, and the ongoing debates surrounding its use in warfare.

The Manhattan Project: The Top Secret Program That Produced the Atomic Bomb in World War II

The Manhattan Project was a highly secretive research program that aimed to develop atomic bombs during World War II. While its primary objective was to end the war, the moral implications of creating such destructive weapons were evident to those involved.

The Ethical and Moral Dilemmas Faced by Scientists Involved in the Manhattan Project

Scientists, including prominent figures like Albert Einstein, grappled with the ethical implications of their work. They were torn between the desire to protect their country and the knowledge that their inventions could inflict immense suffering and death upon civilians.

The Environmental Consequences and Long-Term Effects of the Atomic Bomb

The detonation of the atomic bombs in Hiroshima and Nagasaki had devastating immediate effects, causing widespread destruction and loss of life. However, the long-term environmental consequences, such as radiation sickness and genetic mutations, raised ethical questions about the use of nuclear weapons.

The Political and Diplomatic Implications of the Manhattan Project for Post-War International Relations

The successful development and use of atomic bombs by the United States had profound political and diplomatic implications. It solidified the country's position as a global superpower and shaped the dynamics of the post-war world, leading to the arms race between the United States and the Soviet Union during the Cold War.

The Legacy and Ongoing Debates Surrounding the Manhattan Project and the Use of Atomic Weapons in Warfare

Even decades after the end of World War II, the legacy of the Manhattan Project and the use of atomic weapons continue to spark intense debates. Scholars, policymakers, and the general public still grapple with the moral and ethical questions raised by the project, such as the justifiability of targeting civilians and the potential catastrophic consequences of future nuclear conflicts.

In conclusion, the subchapter "The Moral and Ethical Implications of Nuclear Weapons" offers historians a comprehensive exploration of the profound moral and ethical dilemmas faced by scientists involved in the Manhattan Project. It also delves into the consequences of the atomic bomb, both immediate and long-term, and provides insight into the ongoing debates surrounding the use of atomic weapons in warfare.

The Role of the Manhattan Project in Shaping Public Opinion

The Manhattan Project, the top-secret program that produced the atomic bomb during World War II, played a significant role in shaping public opinion during and after the war. This subchapter delves into the various aspects of this influence, exploring the ways in which the project impacted public perception, ethical dilemmas, political implications, and long-term consequences.

One of the key factors in shaping public opinion was the scientific discoveries and breakthroughs that emerged from the Manhattan Project. The project brought together brilliant minds like Albert Einstein and other prominent scientists, who were instrumental in developing the atomic bomb. Their involvement captured the imagination of the public, as the project became synonymous with scientific progress and technological advancement.

However, the project also raised ethical and moral dilemmas for the scientists involved. The immense destructive power of the atomic bomb forced them to confront the potential consequences of their work. This subchapter explores the inner struggles and debates that these scientists faced, providing insights into the complex choices they had to make.

The espionage and intelligence operations surrounding the Manhattan Project further contributed to its impact on public opinion. As news of the project leaked out, the public became aware of the race between the United States and Nazi Germany to develop atomic weapons. This heightened sense of urgency and competition intensified public support for the project, as it became seen as a necessary means to ensure victory in the war.

The end of World War II marked a turning point in the project's influence. The atomic bomb's devastating impact on Hiroshima and Nagasaki had profound political and diplomatic implications for post-war international relations. It solidified the United States as a world power and set the stage for the Cold War and the arms race between the United States and the Soviet Union.

The long-term effects of the atomic bomb, both environmentally and politically, are also explored in this subchapter. The environmental consequences of nuclear testing and the ongoing debates surrounding the use of atomic weapons in warfare are discussed, shedding light on the lasting legacy of the Manhattan Project.

In conclusion, this subchapter delves into the multifaceted role of the Manhattan Project in shaping public opinion. From the scientific breakthroughs and ethical dilemmas to the political implications and long-term consequences, the project's influence on history is far-reaching and continues to be the subject of ongoing debates. Historians and enthusiasts of the Manhattan Project will find this subchapter to be a comprehensive exploration of the project's impact on public perception and the world at large.

Nuclear Disarmament Movements and Non-Proliferation Efforts

The development and use of atomic bombs during World War II through the Manhattan Project marked a turning point in human history. The destructive power of these weapons brought about a new era of global tensions and concerns about the potential annihilation of humanity. In the aftermath of the war, nuclear disarmament movements and non-proliferation efforts emerged as crucial responses to the dangers of nuclear weapons.

The devastation caused by the bombings of Hiroshima and Nagasaki led to a profound moral and ethical dilemma for the scientists involved in the Manhattan Project. Many of them, including prominent figures like Albert Einstein, became advocates for nuclear disarmament and spoke out against the further use and development of atomic weapons. Their voices played a key role in raising public awareness and fostering global discussions on the need for arms control.

The formation of organizations such as the Committee for Nuclear Disarmament and the Pugwash Conferences on Science and World Affairs in the 1950s and 1960s further galvanized the movement. These groups brought together scientists, policymakers, and activists to discuss the dangers of nuclear proliferation and explore ways to achieve disarmament. Their efforts laid the foundation for the Treaty on the Non-Proliferation of Nuclear Weapons (NPT), which was signed in 1968 and remains the cornerstone of international non-proliferation efforts today.

The NPT aimed to prevent the spread of nuclear weapons to other countries while promoting disarmament among the existing nuclear powers. It established a framework for international cooperation, verification, and monitoring of nuclear activities. However, the treaty also highlighted the unequal power dynamics among nations and the challenges of balancing national security interests with global disarmament goals.

Despite the progress made through the NPT, the world continues to grapple with the threat of nuclear weapons. The end of the Cold War brought renewed hopes for disarmament, with significant reductions in the nuclear arsenals of the United States and Russia. However, the proliferation of nuclear technology to other countries, such as North Korea and Iran, has posed new challenges to non-proliferation efforts.

As historians, it is essential to study and understand the nuclear disarmament movements and non-proliferation efforts that emerged in the wake of the Manhattan Project. By examining the historical context, the ethical dilemmas faced by scientists, and the political and diplomatic implications, we can gain valuable insights into the complex issues surrounding nuclear weapons today. Furthermore, exploring the legacy and ongoing debates surrounding the Manhattan Project can inform current discussions on the use of atomic weapons in warfare and the future of nuclear disarmament.

The Future of Nuclear Technology and the Quest for Peace

As historians, we have a unique perspective on the Manhattan Project, the top-secret program that produced the atomic bomb during World War II. We have delved into the scientific discoveries and breakthroughs that took place, and we have examined the role of prominent scientists like Albert Einstein in this monumental endeavor. We have also explored the ethical and moral dilemmas faced by the scientists involved, as well as the espionage and intelligence operations that surrounded the project.

Now, let us turn our attention to the future of nuclear technology and the quest for peace. The atomic bomb, developed during the Manhattan Project, forever changed the course of history. Its devastating power brought an end to World War II, but it also ushered in a new era of uncertainty and fear.

The environmental consequences and long-term effects of the atomic bomb are still being felt today. The devastation caused by the bombings of Hiroshima and Nagasaki serve as a stark reminder of the destructive potential of nuclear weapons. The race between the United States and Nazi Germany to develop atomic weapons during the war added another layer of urgency to the project, highlighting the political and diplomatic implications it had for post-war international relations.

The Manhattan Project's influence on the Cold War and the arms race between the United States and the Soviet Union cannot be overstated. The fear of mutually assured destruction led to a tense standoff that lasted for decades. The legacy of the Manhattan Project and the ongoing debates surrounding the use of atomic weapons in warfare continue to shape our world.

However, amidst this legacy of destruction and fear, there is hope for a different future. The quest for peace must now be intertwined with the development of nuclear technology. The scientific community has a responsibility to ensure that nuclear power is harnessed for the betterment of humanity and not for destruction.

International cooperation and disarmament efforts are crucial in this endeavor. Treaties like the Treaty on the Non-Proliferation of Nuclear Weapons have paved the way for a more peaceful world. However, there is still much work to be done. The potential for accidental or intentional nuclear disasters remains a looming threat.

As historians, it is our duty to not only study the past but also to shape the future. By examining the impact of the Manhattan Project and the atomic bomb, we can contribute to the ongoing dialogue surrounding nuclear technology and its role in our world. Let us not forget the lessons of history and work towards a future where the quest for peace is at the forefront of nuclear advancements.

9 798223 774549